THE POTAWATOMI

SUZANNE POWELL

THE POTAWATOMI

Franklin Watts   A Division of Grolier Publishing
New York   London   Hong Kong   Sydney   Danbury, Connecticut
A First Book

To my sons, David, Eric, and Ben,
for your love, patience, and understanding.

To all of my students, present and past,
for inspiring me to continue learning and sharing.

To T.C. in Wisconsin for
the beautiful sunsets and inspiring words.

Map by Joe LeMonnier
Photographs ©: Courtesy of American Museum of Natural History: 33 left; Ben
Klaffke: cover, 21, 22, 25 left, 29, 31, 34, 44, 48, 49, 51, 52, 53, 55, 57: North
Wind Picture Archives: 10, 13, 15, 38; Reinhard Brucker: 3, 17, 25 right, 33 right,
36, 42; Tippecanoe County Historical Association, Lafayette, IN: 12, 19, 40, 47;
UPI/Corbis-Bettmann: 26.

Library of Congress Cataloging-in-Publication Data
Powell, Suzanne I.
The Potawatomi / by Suzanne Powell

p. cm. — (A first book)
Includes bibliographical references and index.
Summary: Describes the history and customs of the Potawatomi people.
ISBN 0-531-20268-2 (lib. bdg.) — ISBN 0-531-15888-8 (pbk.)
1. Potawatomi Indians—Juvenile literature. [1. Potawatomi Indians. 2.
Indians of North America.] I. Title. II. Series.
E99.P8P89 1997
305.897'3—dc21   96–52133
                                                          CIP
                                                          AC

CONTENTS

DEDICATION TO THE POTAWATOMI

Land of the lakes
Providing food and pathways
For these people
The first inhabitants.

Master builders
Paddling to uninhabited places
In birch bark canoes
In search of new hunting grounds.

Horticulturists
Carefully planting seeds of life
Sending prayers for rain
Awaiting bountiful harvests.

Fur traders
Allies to those arriving from other lands
Using masterful hunting skills
In exchange for weapons of iron.

Believers
Forced away by others
Holding onto their faith
As the world and its people forever change.

—Suzanne Powell

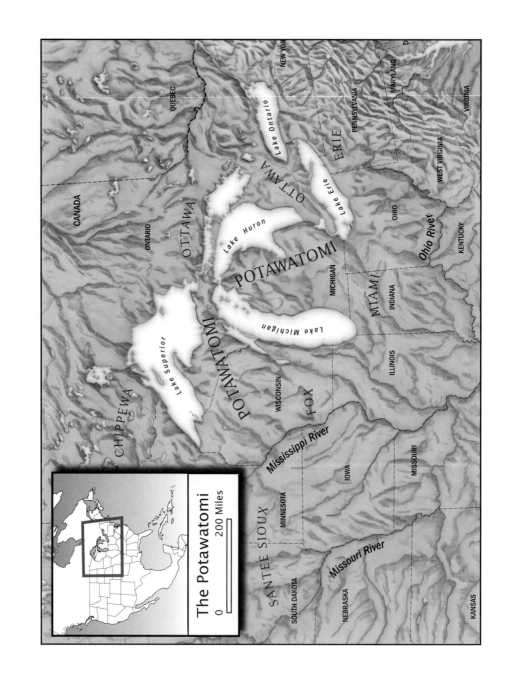

The Potawatomi

0   200 Miles

INTRODUCTION

In the beginning, there lived a large group of Indians who called themselves "Neshnabe" (pronounced nish-NAY-bay), meaning "original people." The Potawatomi were part of this group, which resided along the gulf of the St. Lawrence River near the Atlantic Ocean.

The Neshnabe believed that the people were created by Gitchie Manito, the God of Great Miracles. Gitchie Manito planned for the Neshnabe people to migrate westward. A sacred shell called the Megis shell became the guide for this journey. Whenever the Megis shell appeared to the Neshnabe people, they would move farther west.

Gitchie Manito assigned a special task to each tribe to aid in their survival. The first group, the Ottawa, were assigned the task of providing food and supplies. They were soon known as the "trader people." The

THE POTAWATOMI LIVED ALONG THE RIVERS AND
STREAMS OF THE GREAT LAKES REGION, SUCH AS THE
FOX RIVER IN WISCONSIN.

second group, called the Ojibwa or Chippewa, were
assigned the task of keeping the religion alive. They
soon became known as "keepers of the faith." The
third group, the Potawatomi, were assigned the task
of keeping the fires burning, so they took the name
"keepers of the fire." These groups eventually settled
in the upper and lower peninsulas of Michigan.

HISTORY

Through the research of archaeologists, we know that before A.D. 1500, the ancestors of the Neshnabe people lived north of Lake Huron and Lake Superior. During the next hundred years, they migrated south into the lower peninsula of Michigan along the shores of Lake Michigan. They were very skilled at hunting, fishing, and gathering natural plants. The Neshnabe were known as foragers because they collected the food they needed for survival from their natural environment. This included fish from the waters and animals from the forests. When the plant and animal resources began to diminish, the Neshnabe would move to another location to live.

The neighbors of the Neshnabe in the lower peninsula of Michigan were the Sac and the Fox. These tribes shared their skill at planting and harvesting corn, beans, and squash. In exchange, the

THIS PAINTING BY GEORGE WINTER SHOWS A POTAWATOMI CAMP AT CROOKED CREEK, NEAR LOGANSPORT, INDIANA, IN 1837. WINTER NOTED THAT THEIR NEEDS WERE VERY SIMPLE—A FIRE, A TENT, AND COLORFUL BLANKETS.

Neshnabe shared their knowledge of the building and navigating of bark canoes. As the Neshnabe became farmers, they began to lead a more settled life. Their population increased, and many villages were established within their tribe. A council of elderly leaders, the wkamek (wuh KA mek), managed the activities for all of the villages.

The Neshnabe began hearing stories from others who had traveled east about the arrival of creatures who appeared to be human but had thick hair on their faces. It was said that these "Hairy Faces" possessed tools with magical powers.

A FRENCH-CANADIAN FUR TRAPPER, OR "HAIRY FACE," AS THE POTAWATOMI CALLED THEM

It wasn't long before the Neshnabe had their first encounter with the "Hairy Faces." In the 1600s, the Neshnabe met the first French explorers, led by Jean Nicolet. When Nicolet saw the Neshnabe, he asked who they were. The Huron Indians, who were serving as guides to Nicolet and his band of French explorers, answered that the Neshnabe were makers of fire. The French misunderstood their response and wrote down in their diaries that the Neshnabe were "Pouutouatami." The spelling of this name had changed many times over the years until it became "Potawatomi."

The mission of these French explorers was to open the western Great Lakes to French trade. They became friends with the Potawatomi, supplying them with iron tools, cooking utensils, glass beads, cloth blankets, and firearms. In return, the Potawatomi hunted and provided the French with valuable furs.

In 1641, the Potawatomi were forced from their Michigan lands by Iroquoian tribes from the northeastern part of the United States. They traveled by canoe along the shores of Lake Michigan and up into the northern parts of Wisconsin. In their travels, the Potawatomi met up with some old neighbors, the Sac, Fox, and Kickapoo. They worked hard to rebuild their lives among others who already lived in these new lands, transporting their goods and valuables in canoes.

WHEN THE POTAWATOMI WERE DRIVEN FROM MICHIGAN BY THE IROQUOIS, THEY MOVED INTO AREAS OF NORTHERN WISCONSIN. THEY FOUND BEAUTIFUL NEW PLACES THERE, SUCH AS POST LAKE.

In 1653, the Iroquois reappeared to try to destroy the tribes of northeastern Wisconsin. The Potawatomi heard of this plan and united with other Indian tribes to plan their defense. They built a large village called Mitchigami, meaning "great lake," on the eastern shore of the Door Peninsula in Wisconsin. Mitchigami served as a strong fort that the Iroquois could not penetrate. The Iroquois, lacking food and supplies, soon agreed to a cease-fire.

The united Indian tribes offered to share a feast of food with the Iroquois to celebrate the end of the war. But during the feast, poisoned corn was served to their starving enemies. Many Iroquoians died; those who survived fled to their homeland. Twice more the Iroquois returned to try to defeat the Potawatomi and their united defenders, but they did not succeed.

The Potawatomi tribes continued to expand into many other areas, including places along the Mississippi River. They continued their friendship and trading with the French. The Potawatomi helped the French fight wars against the Iroquois, the Fox, and the Mascoutens. When the English were trying to take over the land and dominate the fur trade, the Potawatomi fought on the side of the French to keep control of the land. Despite the help of the Potawatomi and other Indian tribes, the French were unable to resist the English expansion. The Potawatomi were sad to see their French friends leave, and they attempted to make friends with the English.

In the late 1600s and early 1700s, white settlers from Europe arrived to live in North America. These colonists had come to the new land to make their own laws and be free of English rule. The king of England sent an army across the Atlantic Ocean, hoping to force the colonists to obey the rules of England. The colonists resisted; this led to the Revolutionary War, fought from 1775 to 1783.

AS THE POTAWATOMI MOVED WEST, THEY KEPT
UP A TRADE OF MANY ITEMS WITH THE FRENCH.

The Potawatomi, who had made friends with the English, fought with them during the war. But the colonists won the war, and the land that they were settling came to be called the United States of America. Now the Potawatomi had to deal with the U.S. government, not the French or the English. The English tried one more time to take the land back from the colonists in the War of 1812. The Potawatomi again fought with the English but were not successful. This was the end of any power the English had in the United States. The U.S. government now controlled the land and began making rules about its use.

The 1800s were a devastating time for the American Indians. The government had decided that if the American Indians could not be made to accept the ways of white society, they would have to be moved off their lands. Missionaries were sent by the government to live with Indian groups to try to change their religious beliefs and ways of life. Indian children were taken from their families and put in boarding schools.

While Thomas Jefferson was President of the United States (1801–1809), the government attempted to integrate American Indians into white society. Some people felt that Indian traditions and cultures were inferior and unacceptable in the white

WEWISSA WAS ONE OF SEVERAL YOUNG POTAWATOMI CHIEFS DURING THE 1830S, WHEN HIS PEOPLE WERE BEING REMOVED TO KANSAS. HE IS WEARING A FROCK COAT SIMILAR TO THOSE WORN BY PROSPEROUS WHITE SETTLERS AT THE TIME, BUT HE HAS ADDED SASHES AND A HEAD SCARF, MORE TRADITIONAL CLOTHING ITEMS IN BRIGHT COLORS.

society. But the American Indians were proud people and stood by their heritage. The government's response was to remove all Indians from lands where white people wanted to live. Many white people thought the American Indians were a dying race that soon would no longer exist. By 1817, when James Monroe was president, removal policies were being tried everywhere. Hundreds of Indians were being herded west in an effort to clear the land for the white settlers.

The American government, under the leadership of Andrew Jackson, passed the Forced Removal Bill in 1830. Under this bill, all Indian people still living east of the Mississippi River would be moved west of the river. Indian people did not want to be forced from their homes, and many groups fought for survival.

In 1833, to comply with the Treaty of Chicago, the Potawatomi surrendered all of their lands, about five million acres, to the U.S. government. In return, the government promised to pay the Potawatomi tribes for this land. Many, however, were never paid.

By 1836, most of the Potawatomi people had been forced to move to reservations located in areas that would become the states of Kansas, Iowa, and Oklahoma. Some families refused to move; they fled north into Wisconsin and Canada and hid in the woods. Other Michigan tribes remained in Michigan

THIS EARLY PHOTOGRAPH SHOWS A POTAWATOMI
WOMAN AND HER CHILD ON THE RESERVATION IN
OKLAHOMA. THE PEOPLE WHO HAD BEEN MOVED
CONTINUED TO KEEP ELEMENTS OF THEIR TRADITION,
SUCH AS THE ELABORATE PATTERNS SEEN HERE IN THE
WOMAN'S ROBE AND THE BABY'S CRADLEBOARD.

The United States of America.

To all to whom these Presents shall come, GREETING:

Whereas, There has been deposited in the General Land Office of the United States a schedule of allotments of land, dated *Sept. 15, 1891*, from the Commissioner of Indian Affairs, approved by the Secretary of the Interior *Sept. 15, 89*, whereby it appears that under the provisions of the Act of Congress approved February 8, 1887, (24 Stats. 388,) as amended, by the Act of Congress of March 3, 1891, (26 Stats. 1019,) *Josephine Bourassa*, an Indian of the *Citizen Pottawatomie* tribe or band, has been allotted the following described land, viz:

The West half of Section twenty-eight, in township six North of Range four East of the Indian Meridian, Oklahoma Territory, containing three hundred and twenty acres.

Now, Know Ye, That the United States of America, in consideration of the premises and in accordance with ... the fifth section of said Act of Congress ... 8th February, 1887, HEREBY DECLARES that it does and will hold the land thus allotted (subject to all the restrictions and conditions contained in said fifth section) for the period of twenty-five years, in trust for the sole use and benefit of the said *Josephine Bourassa*, or in case of *her* decease, for the sole use of *her* heirs, according to the laws of the State or Territory where such land is located, and that at the expiration of said period the United States will convey the same by patent to said Indian, or *his* heirs, as aforesaid, in fee, discharged of said trust and free of all charge or incumbrance whatsoever. Provided, That the President of the United States may, in his discretion, extend the said period.

In Testimony Whereof, I, *Benjamin Harrison*, President of the United States of America, have caused these letters to be made Patent and the seal of the General Land Office to be hereunto affixed.

Given under my hand at the City of Washington, this *nineteenth* day of *January*, in the year of our Lord one thousand eight hundred and *Ninety-two*, and of the Independence of the United States the one hundred and *sixteenth*.

By the President: *Benjamin Harrison*

By *C. Shepherd Lacy Ass't* Secretary.

THIS PAPER IS A LAND GRANT DESCRIBING THE PLOT OF
LAND ASSIGNED TO "AN INDIAN OF THE CITIZEN
POTTAWATOMIE TRIBE" IN 1891.

and camouflaged themselves with the Ottawa and Ojibwa people.

One of the bloodiest decades for the American Indians occurred from 1850 to 1860. The size of the territory where the Indians had once lived was cut in half. Two-thirds of their population was destroyed as a result of the Indian wars. Chiefs of many different tribes signed treaties to prevent the destruction of their people.

After the end of the Civil War in 1865, the U.S. government wrote a new Indian policy. There were to be no more treaties or wars. The policy now stated that all American Indians would be living on lands with boundaries, called reservations. The government would have total control over these reservations, providing food, clothing, and other necessities for the American Indians.

By 1890, nearly every tribe was assigned to a reservation by the government. Reservation life was harsh, and the people who lived there felt a loss of hope. For the Potawatomi, the long history of moving from one region to another had ended. Ever since, they have struggled to maintain elements of their traditional lifestyle.

FOOD

Before the arrival of the Europeans in the Americas, the Potawatomi were collectors and gatherers of animals and plants for food. They would move from place to place with the seasons in order to allow these resources to replenish themselves.

The Potawatomi learned farming techniques from neighboring tribes. The responsibility of the women in the tribe was to plant, nurture, and harvest the crops. They raised beans, peas, squash, tobacco, melons, and corn. Most surplus crops were dried and stored for the winter. The rest were used for trading purposes.

As the Potawatomi became better farmers, they began to live a more settled lifestyle. They established villages near their crops and only left the villages during long winter hunts. The Potawatomi would seek

THE POTAWATOMI FARMED SOME CROPS SUCH
AS SUMMER SQUASH (LEFT) AND GATHERED
OTHER NATURALLY-GROWING FOODS SUCH AS
WILD RICE (RIGHT).

out new sites for their villages every ten to twelve years, when the nutrients from the soil were depleted and crops were no longer plentiful.

The Potawatomi, as well as other tribes of the Great Lakes, enjoyed the taste of a seed-bearing grass called wild rice. This grass grew naturally in the streams

TO HARVEST WILD RICE, ONE PERSON POLES THE CANOE
THROUGH THE RICE STAND WHILE ANOTHER PERSON
GENTLY TAPS THE GRAIN STALKS WITH FLAILS SO THAT
THE RICE FALLS INTO THE CANOE.

and marshes in the Great Lakes region and as far west as the Mississippi River. They harvested the grain from their canoes. Wild rice was an important part of their diet. They also used it to trade with neighboring tribes who did not have access to the marshlands.

Tobacco, though not a food item, was an important plant to the Potawatomi. They believed it was a gift from the spirits. The Potawatomi made frequent offerings to thank the spirits for this plant. Before they began a wild rice harvest, for example, they would toss a few pinches of dried tobacco leaves on the waters to ensure ample pickings.

Tobacco was also used in special rituals to establish relations between people. A pinch of tobacco was placed in the stone bowl of a long, feather-decorated pipe called a calumet. Peace treaties between tribes were sealed by the passing and smoking of this sacred pipe.

Throughout the year, both men and women fished in the lakes. Every autumn, men, women, and children all went into the woods for the winter hunt. They did not return until spring. Buffalo hunting provided them with a good supply of meat and skins for the winter months.

The Potawatomi used their knowledge of animal habitats to help them find nuts and berries. The deer mouse, for example, gathers, shells, and stores nuts for the winter. The Potawatomi observed this activity; they waited for the first snow and then searched out the storage places of these small animals.

Along with what they hunted and gathered, the Potawatomi ate "fene," which was made from the nut of the beech tree. The nuts were roasted and pounded into flour for breads and other foods.

They ate a soup that was made with wild rice and blueberries. Another soup was made from cattail roots. This plant was also eaten raw or dried and pounded into flour for bread. They made puddings from pumpkins and squash, or from popped corn and chestnuts. They added maple syrup to many foods for flavor.

When food was plentiful, the Potawatomi would plan special feasts. The feasts were given for a variety of reasons, such as success in hunting or welcoming of strangers. The meal would consist of four courses: the first platter contained two white fish boiled in water; the second served boiled tongue and breast meat of a deer; the third platter had two wood hens, the hind feet of a bear, and the tail of a beaver; and the fourth course was a large quantity of broth made from several kinds of meat. Maple syrup was mixed with water to make a sweet drink that was served with the meal.

NUTS WERE AN IMPORTANT WINTER
FOOD FOR THE POTAWATOMI. THEY
COULD BE POUNDED INTO FLOUR WITH
A STONE MORTAR AND PESTLE.

The Potawatomi valued the resources provided by the lands and water around them. They never took more than they needed of the plants and animals. Instead, they shared with others their gifts from the land.

CLOTHING

The Potawatomi dressed simply. The men wore red or blue cloth in the summer months. In the winter, they would put on highly ornamented buffalo robes. They also wore leggings made of skin or cloth during winter months or special dances. When playing games, such as lacrosse, the men would wear only breechclouts and deerskin moccasins. The Europeans arrived wearing cloth shirts. The Potawatomi preferred wearing these cloth shirts to the leather ones made from the hides of animals.

The women wore dresses that came down to about knee length. They wore a sort of petticoat underneath the dresses which covered them from the waist down to the midleg. Some of the Potawatomi women wore little bonnets, while others covered their heads when traveling with a cowl that was attached to the dress or robe.

TO MAKE A BUFFALO ROBE, THE TANNERS START
WITH A FULL HIDE FROM THE ANIMAL.

The Potawatomi made many clothing items from the hides of animals; they used special tools to tan the hides for use in garments. The tanning process was the work of the women in the tribe.

The tanners began by placing the fresh skin of an animal over a log that was tilted up at one end. Using a scraper made from the sharpened shin bone of a deer, they removed any flesh that still clung to the underside of the skin. Then they washed the hide and left it to soak for several days. This loosened the hair.

The hide was then put back on the log and the remaining hair was scraped off.

The brains of large animals were saved to be used in the next step of the tanning process. The tanners cooked the brains with fat and then rubbed the mixture into the hide. They left the hides like this overnight, allowing the mixture to soak into the skin. The next day, they wrung out the hide and stretched it on a frame built between two close-standing trees. Then they rubbed the whole surface with a stone or bone-headed tool. This left the hide dry and soft.

The final step in the tanning process was smoking the hide. The tanners sewed the hide so that it formed a cone-shaped bag and inverted it over a smoky "smudge fire." The smoke turned the skin a yellow-brown to dark brown color, depending on how long the smoking process lasted.

The tanned hides were then cut and finished with as little sewing as possible. Women wore simple skirts and sleeveless dresses that draped over their shoulders, held in place with a belt. If they needed to sew pieces together, they first had to punch holes through the skin with a bone awl. They used thread made from a plant fiber to hold the skins together. The leggings for the men had strips of hide for use as ties in several places down each leg, so they didn't require any sewing.

THE TANNERS RUB A FAT MIXTURE INTO THE HIDE TO SOFTEN
IT (LEFT). AFTER IT HAS BEEN TREATED, THE HIDE IS STRETCHED
ONTO A FRAME (RIGHT).

THE ORNAMENTS
ON A FINISHED
BUFFALO ROBE
ARE VERY
COLORFUL AND
ELABORATE.
THESE PEOPLE
PROUDLY
DISPLAY THEIR
CEREMONIAL
ROBES AT A
POWWOW.

Both the men and women of the tribe greased their hair and painted their skin. The women usually painted their faces with vermilion, a bright shade of red. The men painted themselves all over for special events, such as lacrosse games. Men also tattooed their bodies with all sorts of designs.

TRANSPORTATION

Living along the coastline of the Great Lakes, the Potawatomi depended on their birch bark canoes as a means of travel and transporting their belongings. American Indians in other parts of the United States used canoes made of sturdier materials, but the birch bark canoe made by Great Lakes Indians is surprisingly strong.

The canoe makers of the Potawatomi tribe began by selecting a tall, straight tree that had tough bark and few knots. While cutting the tree down, the men were very careful not to bruise or damage the trunk. After carefully examining the trunk, they made a mark near each end of the log, about 18 feet (5.5 m) apart. They cut through the bark all around the trunk at each mark and made an incision lengthwise down the trunk.

THE INTRICATE FRAMEWORK OF THIS BIRCH
BARK CANOE IS VISIBLE ON THE INSIDE. LEANING
AGAINST THE CANOE ARE TWO PADDLES FORMED
FROM LARGE PIECES OF BARK.

The carvers lifted the log up on other supporting logs, then peeled back the bark from the incision and pried it away from the log. Then they pushed it downward and off with great care so that it would not buckle or tear. Spring or summer is the best time to remove the bark, because it is easier to peel when it's moist.

The next step in the process was to flatten the bark. This required the use of a torch made from pieces of the dry outer bark, called waste bark, inserted into a split stick. The canoe makers set the flame of the torch against the moist, inner side of the canoe bark. If they applied the flame evenly, the bark would flatten out like a blanket. Then they laid the flattened bark out on the ground, outer side up, and rolled it into a bundle while they built the frame for the canoe.

In creating the canoe's framework, it was necessary to achieve the proper shape so that the bark covered the frame properly. Long pieces of a straight-grained wood such as cedar became the gunwales, ribs, and sheathing.

Each canoe had about four dozen bent ribs. These pieces of wood were two fingers thick, that is, about an inch and a half (4 cm), and three to four inches (7.5 to 10 cm) wide. The canoe makers made the ribs flexible by boiling them. Then they bent the wood to the right shape and tied it down until it dried.

The gunwales, the long strips that gave the canoe its shape at the top, were shaped carefully with an upward bend at each end. The ribs fit against the gunwales and were held in place by three crossbars made of tough wood.

"THE SILENT FISHERMAN," A DRAWING BY
N. C. WYETH, SHOWS A CANOE WITH A LARGE
DESIGN PAINTED ON ONE END. THIS WAS THE
CANOE MAKER'S "SIGNATURE."

In preparing for the construction of the canoe, the Potawatomi built a form of stakes; they drove the stakes into the ground around the framework in the shape of the canoe. As soon as the bark was placed within the framing stakes, the work of fastening the gunwales began. Each step continued until the ribs were each securely wedged in place. An expert builder placed the bark sheathing over the ribs. It was difficult to fasten because it would frequently split at the ends. On early canoes, the wood and bark were pierced with awls and sewn together with tough roots.

When the builders finished the canoe, they took it from its frame and inverted it. Finally, they gummed the seams in the bark with pitch. They left the canoe to dry. If the canoe maker wanted his product to be unique, he would paint eyes or other figures at each end of the canoe. Such designs were the craftsman's signature.

The Potawatomi moved often, either to seek out more fertile land for farming or to flee from other attacking tribes. They used the birch bark canoes to move all their possessions.

With the arrival of the Europeans came a new form of transportation. Following the victory of the British in the French and Indian War in 1755, the Potawatomi gathered up more than two hundred horses from those slain in the war. Within a few years, the Potawatomi began to rely more on their horses for transportation

THE POTAWATOMI FOUND THAT HORSES WERE A RELIABLE MEANS OF TRANSPORTATION. THESE HORSES AT AN ENCAMPMENT ARE BEING HOBBLED—THEIR LEGS ARE LOOSELY FASTENED TOGETHER SO THAT THEY DO NOT RUN AWAY IN THE NIGHT.

than their birch bark canoes. The horses were more rugged and reliable and allowed the Potawatomi quick transportation across land.

With the horses as transportation, the Potawatomi soon started crossing the Mississippi River to hunt, and they traveled into Missouri and Iowa. By the early 1800s, only a few Potawatomi tribes around the southern end of Lake Michigan and along the nearby rivers relied on their canoes.

DWELLINGS

The villages and campsites of the Potawatomi were usually located along rivers, streams, or the larger lakes. It was these waterways that provided transportation and good sources of food.

The Great Lakes tribes had three different kinds of dwellings: dome-shaped, cone-shaped, and rectangular. The dome-shaped dwelling was used most often by the Potawatomi because it was easy to build and transport. They built the structure with an oval or circular shape.

The builders collected saplings from trees and bushes and pushed them into the ground to form the shape of the dwelling. Then they bent the tops of the saplings in toward the center and twisted and locked them together to form an arc at the top. They attached more saplings horizontally all the way around the structure to reinforce the frame. They covered the

THIS DOME-SHAPED
DWELLING IS COVERED
WITH BIRCH BARK.

frame with bark from birch, ash, elm, spruce, or cedar trees. Each dwelling would provide shelter for about four people comfortably. Some were larger, to house more family members. When it came time to move, the Potawatomi could simply uproot the structure and place it on rush mats, then drag it to its new place.

Low benches were arranged around the inside of the dome-shaped dwelling for use as beds. Sticks and brush were placed on top of the benches and then covered by animal fur, hides, or mats made by the women. A hole in the center of the dome roof allowed smoke from a fire in the middle of the dwelling to escape. The hole also allowed light inside.

In the summer months, the Potawatomi, and other Great Lakes tribes, would construct large rectangular lodges that provided more space for each person. These structures were cooler during the warm months. Some were large enough to house four or five families. Builders made the frame for such dwellings with saplings, just like those used for the dome dwellings, but set in two long rows that bent in and joined at each end. They bent the saplings inward and twisted them together to form an arc at the top. Then they placed more saplings in the opposite direction to provide support to the framework. They covered the frame with sheets of bark that overlapped like roof shingles. The bark sheets were held in place

THE LARGE SUMMER HOUSES CONTAINED LONG BENCHES THAT
PROVIDED SLEEPING SPACE FOR SEVERAL FAMILIES. THE FRAMEWORK
FOR THE STRUCTURE CONSISTS OF SAPLINGS THAT FORM AN ARCH
PLUS PIECES THAT RUN ALONG THE LENGTH OF THE BUILDING.

by poles and sticks. An opening one to two feet wide (0.3 to 0.6 m) and running the length of the structure was left along the top to let in light and let out smoke from fires. There was room inside to make several fires for cooking and for light during the evening hours. Two families would often share the same fireplace. Food, clothing, skins, and weapons were hung from ceiling poles inside the dwelling.

The Potawatomi needed homes that were comfortable and durable yet still movable. They depended on the land and waterways around them for farming and hunting, but if they stayed in one place too long they would strain these resources. This is why they built each type of dwelling so that it served a purpose for them while they were stationary and could easily be moved when necessary.

RELIGIOUS BELIEFS AND RITUALS

The Potawatomi had organized beliefs and ritual practices. They believed in the concept of a "Great Spirit," and in gods of fire, sea, and sun. They also had a strong belief in the supernatural powers of natural objects such as plants, rocks, and animals. When a death occurred among the Potawatomi, the body would be placed on a scaffold for a certain number of days. The other tribe members conducted a special ceremony to celebrate the departure of the soul or spirit from the deceased person's body. They believed that the spirit of the body would follow a trail over the stars in the Milky Way galaxy toward the west, where it would be admitted into heaven.

One of the religious organizations of the Potawatomi was the Grand Medicine Society. This society served to heal those who were sick. Medicine people used roots, plants, and the bark of different plants to make many medicines. They made a balm

THE POTAWATOMI BELIEVED THAT A PERSON'S SPIRIT
LEFT THE BODY WHEN HE OR SHE DIED. AFTER THE
SPIRIT DEPARTED, THE BODY WAS PLACED IN THE
GROUND AND THE AREA AROUND THE SPOT WAS
CLEARED OF GRASS. THEN A WHITE FLAG WAS PLACED
INTO THE GROUND AS AN EMBLEM OF PEACE.

MEDICINE PEOPLE USED A VARIETY OF MATERIALS
TO HEAL THE SICK, INCLUDING RED WILLOW
BARK (LEFT) AND BUFF BALSAM (RIGHT).

THE RATTLES AND OTHER OBJECTS USED IN CEREMONIAL DANCES ARE BEAUTIFULLY DECORATED.

from the fresh roots of cattail plants to treat burns and wounds. They knew that eating the roots of certain plants would cure a stomachache. They made a tea from milkweed roots as a medicine for several ailments. Many of the medicines used today were first discovered by the Potawatomi and other tribes years ago.

The Potawatomi worked to protect the spirit as well as the body. They conducted ceremonies using medicine bags and other sacred objects to ward off bad or evil spirits. They also held religious ceremonies, in which they danced to the music of drums, whistles, and rattles.

TOOLS

The Potawatomi used bows and arrows, spears, snares, and traps for hunting deer, elk, bear, beaver, muskrats, and other animals. They also fished in the lakes, rivers, and streams around them using hooks, lines, nets, and spears. They made all these tools using the simple materials readily available to them, such as branches, stones, and animal bones.

The women of the tribe used digging sticks and wooden hoes for planting and harvesting crops. Both men and women collected sap from maple trees. They used wooden wedges and troughs to draw the sap from the tree. Then they collected it in birch bark buckets, wooden bowls, or clay pottery. They made the sap into a syrup that they used on almost all their food.

The Potawatomi had many different tools for making food. They used large wooden pestles for pounding corn into meal. Pottery jars, wooden bowls, and ladles were made by the women of the tribe to prepare and serve food.

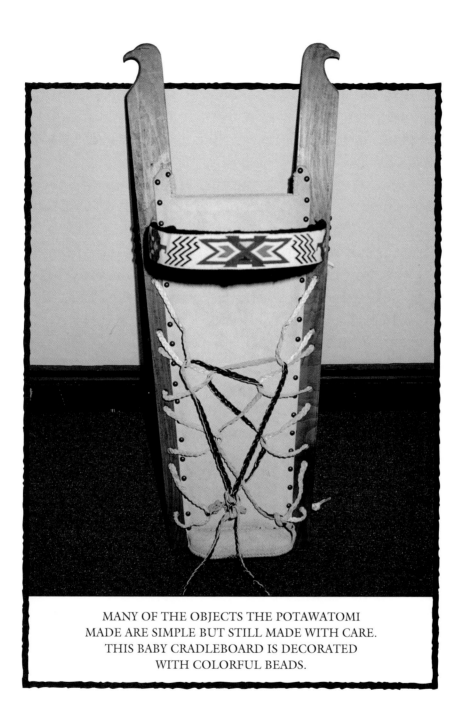

MANY OF THE OBJECTS THE POTAWATOMI
MADE ARE SIMPLE BUT STILL MADE WITH CARE.
THIS BABY CRADLEBOARD IS DECORATED
WITH COLORFUL BEADS.

Grasses and branches could be made into many different things. Bags woven from reeds provided storage for food and other objects. Reed mats served as both chairs and beds inside the dome-shaped dwellings.

During the winter hunting months, people wore snowshoes so that they could travel easily through the deep snow. They also made toboggans and loaded them with supplies when they traveled on foot in the winter.

The musical instruments used in ceremonial rituals included rattles, flutes, whistles, and drums. They could

THIS PIPE, CARVED OUT OF STONE, IS USED IN
MEDICINAL CEREMONIES.

EVERYTHING FROM HOMES TO STONE SCRAPERS ARE MADE
FROM THE MATERIALS NATURE PROVIDES.

be made in a variety of shapes and sizes from heavy plant shoots, roots, gourds, and animal skins. The tobacco pipes used for special ceremonies or rituals were constructed from clay or stone.

The Potawatomi made knives and scrapers from chipped flint. The bones of animals were made into awls. They made every tool, cooking utensil, or weapon by hand from the animals and plants around them. They never wasted what Mother Nature had provided. Instead, the people thanked the Great Spirit for providing them with all they needed for survival.

THE POTAWATOMI TODAY

Starting in the early 1900s, more and more of the Potawatomi people were forced to live on reservations. Their days of moving from one location to another ended, and on the reservations a new way of life was established.

Over the years, many Potawatomi began to find wage-paying work as migrant workers or in industries. Many left the reservations or their jobs in the 1940s to fight in World War II. After the war, many Potawatomi men and their families settled near cities where they could find jobs. Others who stayed on reservations lived in impoverished conditions while trying to maintain their traditional lifestyle. New jobs often required more education than the Potawatomi could get.

Those who remained on reservations continued to make baskets and other crafts to sell. Some of their arts and crafts are admired and in great demand. This has allowed

THE POTAWATOMI ARE VERY SKILLED AT
MAKING MANY ITEMS, SUCH AS THESE
BEADED MOCCASINS.

many American Indians not only to earn a living but also to continue their heritage and share it with others.

The Potawatomi now live in many different places in the Midwest and Plains states. Those who live on reservations and those who still live in the area around the Great Lakes are certainly a part of the modern world. Many have invested in casinos in these areas. The casinos serve as a steady source of income to preserve the reservations.

The Citizens Band of Potawatomi in Oklahoma and the Prairie Band in Kansas also remain strong in number. They continue to hold traditional values and yet find ways to earn a living that allow them to avoid poverty.

Finding the means to educate the children of these tribes has often been a challenge over the years. Public schools have provided one source of education for them. The money that is made from the casinos and other contributions is being used to develop additional educational programs for children. Continuing education is necessary for survival in today's society.

The Potawatomi have joined members of other tribes around the country in ceremonial Powwows. Many of their arts and crafts are made and sold at these special events. More important, though, people from all over the country have the privilege of sharing and learning from these experiences. During the Powwows, members of different groups dress in their elaborate regalia and dance to the music of the drums. Men, women, and children dance together to share their heritage.

For the Potawatomi, it has been a long, difficult struggle to change from a way of life that relied on nature alone to one that demands formal education and jobs for survival. The Potawatomi will continue to pass down their heritage to other generations. It is that very heritage that has allowed them to live in peaceful harmony with a changing world.

THE POWWOW IS AN IMPORTANT ACTIVITY FOR
THE POTAWATOMI. THEY USE THIS TIME TO
SHARE THEIR HERITAGE WITH OTHERS AND PASS
IT ALONG TO THEIR CHILDREN.

GLOSSARY

ancestors people from whom others descend.

archaeologist a scientist who studies the lives of ancient peoples by looking at the materials they have left behind.

awl a small, pointed tool used to make holes in wood or leather.

canoe a narrow, lightweight boat propelled by paddles.

cowl a hood.

firearm a hand weapon such as a rifle or pistol from which a shot is fired by explosive force.

foragers collectors of wild plant foods, animals, and fish.

gunwale the top rim of a canoe or other boat.

heritage tradition handed down from one generation to another.

incision a careful cut.

inferior lower in order or quality.

lacrosse a traditional game played by two teams using a leather ball and long-handled racquets with pouches.

missionaries people sent out to convert others to their religious belief or to conduct humanitarian activities.

nutrients substances that sustain life or promote growth.

pestle a tool used to pound grain into meal or flour.

petticoat a woman's underskirt.

reservations areas of land set aside by the government, to which American Indian groups were encouraged or forced to move.

ritual a set form or system of doing something.

saplings young trees.

scaffold a temporary framework.

sheathing flat material that forms the base for the siding of a canoe or other structure.

stationary not moving; unchanging.

vermilion a bright red pigment.

FOR FURTHER READING

Clifton, James A. *The Potawatomi*. New York: Chelsea House, 1987.

Cunningham, Maggie. *Little Turtle*. Minneapolis: Dillon Press, 1978.

Greene, Jacqueline D. *The Chippewa*. New York: Franklin Watts, 1993.

Kubiak, William J. *Great Lakes Indians*. New York: Bonanza Books, 1970.

Landau, Elaine. *The Ottawa*. Danbury, Conn.: Franklin Watts, 1996.

Oldenburg, E. William. *Potawatomi Indian Summer*. Grand Rapids: Eerdmans, 1975.

Whelan, Gloria. *Night of the Full Moon*. New York: Knopf, 1993.

INDEX

ABOUT THE AUTHOR

Suzanne Powell resides in Grand Rapids, Michigan, with her family. She is an elementary teacher and has a special interest in studying the cultural background of the North American Indian tribes. She is the author of *The Pueblos* for the Franklin Watts Indians of the Americas series. She is also co-author, with Patricia Ryon Quiri, of *Stranger Danger*, published in 1985.